Cookie King, Wally 'Famous' Amos

Mini-Biography of Famous Amos Cookies Founder

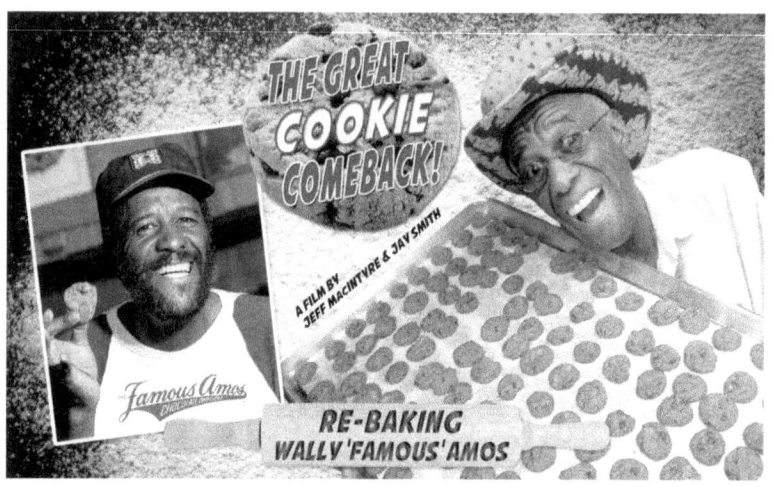

Material for this book came from video interviews with Wally Amos. They were used in the documentary about Wally's life, **The Great Cookie Comeback.**

More film info: www.GreatCookieComeback.com

Cookie King, Wally 'Famous' Amos

Mini-Biography of Famous Amos Cookies Founder

JEFF MacINTYRE

CONTENT MEDIA
GROUP

First published by Content Media Group, LLC

Copyright © 2021 by Jeff MacIntyre

First edition

Table of Contents

Life may look like it crumbles, but life never crumbles. Everything is an opportunity for growth.

Wally Amos

1

Introduction

Be honest, when you were plowing through that bag of Famous Amos Cookies, did you ever contemplate anything more than, "Mmm, me want more cookies!"? Did you ever wonder if there was a real baker named Amos? Of course not. Thinking and savoring chocolate chips don't mix.

Until 2015, I never gave the brand, nor the man, a second thought. Honestly, I could care less about packaged cookies. When my buddy, Jay Smith, moved to Honolulu and crossed paths with the cookie legend, Wally "Famous" Amos, everything changed.

Jay told me about the meeting and we started brainstorming Wally-centric projects. Someone suggested a reality show to follow Wally's adventure of starting another cookie company. Not a fan of the genre, I wasn't feeling it and suggested we do a documentary on his incredible life.

Wally was game! We started rolling cameras on his life in Hawaii, learning about his remarkable past and surprising present.

One of the first shoots with Wally takes place in the kitchen of his Honolulu high-rise apartment, complete with a stunning view of Diamond Head. Jay's filming Wally making a batch of his famous cookies and asks when his love for cookies started.

Wally: "I started making cookies around 1970. I made them for five years before I sold them. At the time, I was an agent and had a client named Shari Summers. [You may remember her from Harold and Maude and Bad News Bears.] She was a wonderful actress. We finished our meeting and she busted out some chocolate chip cookies.

I hadn't had any homemade cookies in a long time. My Aunt Della used to send them to me when I was in the Air Force stationed here in Hawaii. When I tasted them, memories just rushed to my head, and I said, "Shari, where'd you get these cookies from?" She said, "It's just the Nestle Toll House chocolate chip recipe."

As soon as the meeting was over, I went to the nearest supermarket to get all the ingredients. I went home and started making cookies right away, because I was really excited! I'd go to meetings and take cookies with me. I used cookies as my calling card, literally. And developed a nice reputation in Hollywood for making chocolate chip cookies that really tasted great!

There's a shelf somewhere in this cosmic world that has what each of you, each of us, is meant to do, to be. And the shelf with chocolate chip cookies had my name on it. Chocolate chip cookies were my calling."

Ever since I was a teenager, I'd hear people blathering on about the importance of "finding your calling". Self-help gurus make millions on the rally cry. I don't doubt it's importance. Life's too short to get mired in the muck of mediocrity and boredom. BUT, at times, one's "calling" is as elusive as a Skittles-pooping unicorn.

For over 25 years, I've travelled the globe as a producer, cameraman and editor. Telling important stories of marginalized people and underrepresented topics has been life-changing. As I type, it just now hits me, "Was this MY calling?" If it was, my phone must've been in Airplane Mode. I don't remember the –ring-, the call. For me, work with purpose slowly transformed into a passion.

Wally, on the other hand, was almost deafened by the ring. Remember, this was the 70s. No call-waiting. No voicemail. You either pick it up or risk missing the call for good.

When Wally bit down on Shari's homemade cookies, the spotlight switched on, a band started playing, while a skywriter formed the cloudy message, "Cookies are your calling". At least, that's how it feels.

For Wally, the gravitational pull to flour, eggs, sugar and chocolate chips was undeniable. I truly believe cookies were his calling. He could NOT bake and sell cookies. It would've been a denial of destiny. And you don't want to deny destiny. She has a bitter retaliatory streak that can reduce the largest Sumo wrestler to a puddle of blubbery tears.

Wally's early destiny wasn't denied. He leaned in, shattering records, glass ceilings and expectations. Later, however, destiny gets a tad pissy when Wally misses her call. It begs the question, "Like toilet paper, is destiny meant to only be used once?" Or, does one's destiny change as we do?

Keep that in mind, as you immerse yourself in Wally's twisty-turny life story. Is there a moment when, perhaps, he should've pivoted away from cookies? Just because you hit a big jackpot on that one Wheel of Fortune slot machine, doesn't mean Vanna will strike twice.

With every fibre of my being, I'm resisting the urge to type a Kenny Rogers' lyric...but can't. Sorry. You've been warned.

Sing along, because you DO know the words. "Sometimes you got to know when to hold 'em and when to fold 'em." (Something my dry cleaner used to always say.)

Oh, relief.

Did Wally hold on too long? Embedded in Wally's story are gold nuggets for all to grab. Equal parts success story and cautionary tale, his experience shines light on blind spots we all struggle with. This is why I love sharing it. Everyone connects with a piece that resonates just for them. Too foo-foo? Maybe, but keep an open mind and see if you spot yourself in Wally. I know I did.

Since I live in Los Angeles, I had to make the great sacrifice for this film and travel to Hawaii to interview the Cookie King, Wally Amos.

Oh, thank you. Your sympathy is palpable.

What follows are the transcripts from those interviews. They were recorded from 2015-2019; some were shot by my co-producer, Jay Smith. Keep in mind, this isn't a traditional novel or biography. It's the text from our conversations with the cookie legend.

To date, my passport has stamps from 50 countries. From world leaders to celebrities to ancient tribes living in the rainforest, I've met a lot of fascinating characters. During my career, I've probably interviewed more than 650 people, but can unequivocally say, there's only one Wally Amos. He's a true original.

While he may have ripped the recipe from a bag of Nestle Chocolate Chips, his recipe for life is as unique as his DNA. Since there will never be another, you made the right choice to get to know the one and only...
Wally "Famous" Amos.

In case you're interested in seeing/tasting Wally's "secret" cookie recipe, he'd love you to have it!

Grab your free copy here:
www.GreatCookieComeback.com/recipe

2

Look Out World,
Wally is Born!

J eff MacIntyre: Wally, describe your earliest childhood memory?

Wally Amos: At 1AM on July 1, 1936 my scream signaled
the rhythm of life in the only son born to Wallace and
Ruby Amos, and in the tiny two-room house, located
about twenty-five yards from the railroad tracks in the
black section of Tallahassee, Florida.

Happiness and prayers prevailed. But, so did the fact
I was born on the heels of the Great Depression. That
meant my mother, Ruby, couldn't spend too much time
at home recuperating or enjoying her new son, Wallace
Jr. These were hard times. For Ruby and Wallace Sr.,
who couldn't read or write, keeping their jobs came first.

Jeff: Tell me more about your parents.

Wally: Early in my youth, I learned all about my parents: Wallace, Sr. had more bark than bite and Ruby barked the loudest. Plus, she had the biggest bite! She was the chief disciplinarian. All of this disciplining had nothing to do with my being terribly mischievous as a boy.

It was just that Ruby was always firm in her instructions to me--or anyone for that matter. And if her instructions were not followed to the letter, then you might as well be prepared to deal with something you hadn't bargained for.

Despite my advanced knowledge of what could happen if I crossed Ruby, I seemed to make the mistake of challenging her from time to time. And that was not too smart of me, because I would never end up the winner, just the recipient of a sore behind.

It was almost as though Ruby had decided at an early age that she would have to work hard all of her life, and if that was the way it was going to be, then she was going to be the best and hardest worker there was.

Without being able to read or write, the only work for a black woman in the South who didn't live on a farm was as a domestic. That meant Ruby helped support the family by washing someone else's windows, floors, clothes and children. And it didn't matter what Ruby was called upon to do, she would do it with fervor and professionalism.

For that reason alone, Ruby was one of the most in-demand domestics working in Tallahassee-a fact that made her one the highest paid in her field and busiest. It also meant she was absent from her own home for most of the days during the week, something that didn't bother me or Wallace, Sr.

She also seemed to be spending a lot of time away from home, even when she wasn't working. Had I been aware of such things, I would have realized the reason for Wallace's and Ruby's absenteeism was they were becoming incompatible day-by-day. However, I was too young to know about that word, and Ruby and Wallace wouldn't have known what it meant had they heard of it.

As for my father, Wally, Sr., when you get down to it, it's not the name, but what's inside a person that matters most. My father was a good person for a number of reasons. The most apparent was his willingness to always remain true to himself and his station in life. He had no education to speak of, but he was a hardworking man. He was a laborer at the local gas plant, a job he remained at for his entire working life. Wallace wasn't aggressive like Ruby, and he never made an effort to challenge her position of Chief Disciplinarian.

Father and son moments were quite limited between Wallace and me. But, when we did get to spend time together, it was always special for me. No matter what it was--visiting him at the plant and using his Lava soap to take a shower (and almost losing my skin as well), or having him take me for my monthly Saturday haircut--I treasured those moments of being alone with my father. But those moments were rare. Too rare.

I've learned to love and accept 'Mr. Wallace', as he was affectionately called by the kids in the neighborhood, for what he was: a man doing the best he knew how to do with what he had to work with. Although, I wasn't heavily influenced by him. I know I did pick up that latter trait: doing the best I can with what I have to work with.

Summers, I would go to Orlando, Florida to visit my grandmother and aunt. My life kind of revolved around going to church, playing in the yard with a couple of friends, but there was nothing outstanding. It was a pretty routine childhood.

Jeff: How religious were your parents?

Wally: Having both parents working did not deprive me of the southern breeding that comes with being southern born. No matter what the conditions were in the outside world--meaning the world outside of the South--my life was one of strict religious instruction and good manners.

Since Wallace and Ruby were serious about religion, they kept my training in that area continuous. This meant there would be very few fun days, as some people may know them. Anything that appeared to be fun, like dancing, was a sin in the Amos home. Anything that was not part of the tenets of the strict religious diet I was being fed, I had better not do.

Therefore, dancing was something I did not learn to do during those youthful years in Tallahassee. However, there were other things I had to learn and make sure I practiced, or I would pay a high price.

I attended church every Sunday. I was there because Wallace and Ruby insisted upon it, not because my soul needed cleansing. As I got older, and into my early teens, I did have reason for penance because of my thoughts about girls, which I dared not let Ruby find out about. However, as far as Ruby and Wallace were concerned, they were seeing that I got a good Christian education, because it had been ordained early in my youth that my 'calling' was to the pulpit.

However, with all that was predicted, I never got a 'calling' that I could hear to become a preacher man.

Jeff: What was it like to grow up in the segregated South?

Wally: Every level of discrimination was enacted. You name it, and we were in it. We lived in a segregated neighborhood, riding a segregated bus. I remember one experience, it was a Sunday, and my mother and I would visit other churches, primarily to listen to gospel music.

We'd finished the day and came to the bus stop to take the bus, because the church activities were all the way on the other side of town.

The bus was empty. A couple of servicemen were in the back and Ruby got on board and sat in the first seat she saw, because we were walking and she was tired, and it was right up front in the white-only area. The white guys asked the driver to have her move, and she pretended she didn't hear. She just kept sitting there.

Ruby was tired. She'd been walking all over the area of town that we'd been visiting. And she was a very opinionated lady and nobody ever told her what to do, definitely not her son. And I was, I don't know, seven, eight, nine, somewhere in that neighborhood.

Ruby said, "I'm not moving anywhere." The driver made several attempts to get her to move and she was not budging. Also on the bus were a couple black servicemen and they moved a little closer. So, he stopped making an issue of where we were sitting and ultimately decided to leave Ruby alone. She stayed where she was.

Years ago, I was reading something about the lady in Detroit, Rosa Parks. And I thought about Ruby on that day in the bus in Tallahassee, Florida. Time, place different. She could have been the Rosa Parks of our era, because she was not moving.

Jeff: As a child, did you realize was happening?

Wally: You don't realize it, you know it. If you're raised in the South, the law of the land is segregation, then that's what's happening. And you knew that. That was during the height of segregation, so the blacks had no rights.

3

The Life-Changing Move

J eff: You're twelve now and your parents are fighting constantly. Divorce is on the horizon. What happens to you?

Wally: When I think about why I'm in the cookie business, the short of it is: I'm in the cookie business because my mother and father got a divorce. Now, that obviously requires some explanation, but at the age of 12, I was still living in Tallahassee, Florida. My mother and father constantly had disagreements. I guess they'd had one disagreement too many and she decided she and I would move.

She would move to Orlando, Florida, which is where her mom lived and she had a younger sister who lived there. And I would move to New York to live with Aunt Della. And that's exactly what happened.

Jeff: When you found out your Mom was putting you, a twelve year old boy, on a train to New York, what did you think?

Wally: It didn't matter, because we didn't have a very strong family connection. I was looking forward to it. Something different. Something new. Something I've never done before in New York. Where, supposedly there were fewer restrictions on blacks living in New York. I had no fear.

I wasn't a deep thinker, so I wasn't thinking anything. Whatever comes up, comes up. And I didn't have a choice, you know. It wasn't like, "Do you want to go with me to Orlando or do you want to go to New York?" You just get on the train and go to New York. That was my life; doing what I was told and not questioning it.

I remember the enormity of Penn Station. There's people everywhere. Subway ride was a nickel. And Ruby was such a stickler for details. She insisted I take my shoe shine box with me. A little country bumpkin going from Florida to New York City and I get off the train with a shoe shine box.

Aunt Della and Lily picked me up. They laughed at me and told that story for months, maybe years, but that was just a reality of it.

I'm carrying this shoebox with me and nothing could epitomize country more than the black boy getting off the train with his shoe box on his shoulder.

Jeff: What was life with Aunt Della like?

Wally: Living with Aunt Della was a treat because Ruby was a disciplinarian and would hit me with whatever was handy. I used to tell her when she was alive, if she was still living and managed me the way she did in those days, I can have her arrested for child brutality because it really was. But obviously, no, it was a different time and different era.

Aunt Della was just the opposite. Aunt Della was loving, Aunt Della was fun. The thought of hitting me would never occur to Aunt Della, the thought hitting anyone never occurred to Aunt Della.

Jeff: What did you learn from Aunt Della?

Wally: I think being around her helped formulate a tender side of me; a fun side of me, also. I think the fun I see in life, that I have, much of that came from Aunt Della.

We were doing something in the living room one day, I have no idea what we were doing, but I think she offered me two dollars, if I'd kiss her feet. I just loved money, so that was a no brainer. I said, "Sure, I can kiss your feet, Aunt Della." And she gave me two dollars. Little stuff like that.

But the memory I have of Aunt Della is baking cookies. Man, I had never eaten a chocolate chip cookie before Aunt Della. My mother never made cookies. She always made cakes and pies. Aunt Della was the first person that ever made chocolate chip cookies. It was the Toll House recipe.

I can still remember sitting in that small kitchen and her mixing up a batch of chocolate chip cookies, Toll House Cookies. Oh, wow. That had a direct impact on my going into the cookie business, because if she hadn't given me that experience, there never would have been a cookie from Wally Amos. It was because of her making cookies for me, and my developing such a strong love for those cookies, that I wound up going into the cookie business.

So, you never know where it's coming from. You never know when it's coming or how it will impact you. You just need to be open and receptive, because you're always living from your past, you're always living from something you've done before, otherwise there's no today if you don't pick up from yesterday.

There's a shelf somewhere in this cosmic world that has what each of you, each of us, are meant to do, be. And the shelf with chocolate chip cookies has my name on it. That was what I was supposed to do. I never analyzed it, resisted it or wanted to know more details.

When you know more, then what? First of all, it's information that's already happened. It doesn't have any meaning now. Life is constantly changing, all the time. But you have to respond when it happens.

Now. It's always now. The best time to do anything is always now. The best place to do anything is always here. But you know, we want to wait 'until'. You'll die waiting until, because you don't know when until is coming or what it looks like either. You might not even recognize it when it shows up. So, act now. Be here now.

4

The Air Force

D ays before his 17th birthday, July 1st 1953, Wally convinces his mother to allow him to drop out of high school and join The Air Force.

Wally: I quit school before graduating. I was 16 years old and I had to get my mom's permission in order to leave. I did that in the summer of 1953 and by September, it rolled around and they hadn't called me. I had kinda gotten back in my routine and I really didn't want to go when they finally called. But it was too late then.

One day I got that letter, "Greetings, you'll report at 39 Whitehall Street." That's still where people go, military guys go. And so I went. I went to the basic training in Samson, New York, upstate New York. It was so cold there, man. It was so cold that the water in the butt cans would be frozen in the morning and they had no heat anywhere.

It was just disastrous, and they have an exercise doing the obstacle course. And let me tell you, there's some real obstacles on that course. It is appropriately named. But I was a little slick guy. I'd always figure out the easy way to do things. And I'm still able to do that. But I've learned not to look for the easy way, but the best way.

But anyway, we come to this rope that extends from on the decline from the top of this hill, down to the bottom and it's freezing. They give you these leather shells and you had wool gloves that you put in the shell. But you can't grip anything. And I gotta grip this rope, and I gotta wrap my legs around the rope, and I gotta go down the rope backwards.

So, I came up with a brilliant solution, that it isn't gonna take me that long to get to the bottom. I'll take my gloves off, put them in my pocket, and then I'll speed on down that rope head first, which is what I did. And when I got to the bottom my hands were frozen.

I couldn't open them and, oh, was I in misery, but you learn something from every experience. What I learned was that the area right up near your groin between your legs, is the warmest spot of your body. And that's where

I put my hands and thawed them out, but I was hurting for some time after that. Anyway, I finally left Sampson and... [chuckle] Life is very comical and it's very sadistic. It's all of those, but it's the best thing going in spite of all of that.

I went from Sampson Air Force Base to Biloxi, Mississippi and was reminded of all the discrimination, and all the stuff that I had experienced in Tallahassee, Florida. Now, still remember, I'm 17 years old, so I haven't had any experiences really, but I remember those, man.

Part of the reason I joined the Air Force was to fly, be around airplanes and see the world. I soon found out Sampson was not going to make that a reality, not for me or any of the hundreds of other raw, frightened young men like me. Instead, we would spend the the next two months being deprogrammed from our civilian way of life. And the first thing on the agenda was to strip us of all human dignity and make us feel smaller than small.

One way was in the clothing. They would issue you clothing that was far too large for you. And if you complained about what their tailor had issued you, then you could expect to be yelled at regularly. It was their philosophy, the more yelling we experienced, the stronger would be our sense of fear. Hell, I was way ahead of them. Ruby had preceded them by seventeen years.

Jeff: After you complete your training in Biloxi, you set off for Hickam Air Force Base in Honolulu, Hawaii. BUT, you travel by ship from San Francisco. Tell me about that experience.

Wally: That was my first boat ride; sleeping in a hammock. And I was stupid and picked up the habit of gambling. And I gambled shooting dice on the boat over.

I got to Hawaii and didn't have any money left. I was just a little dumb kid. I did stupid things attempting to be cool and looking to fit in. You know, we all want to fit in, because we don't think we're enough.

Hawaii was a reward for enduring the boat ride, Mississippi, and all the other stuff. As time went on, I made friends and loved it, and I acclimated very much.

I think it's so interesting I wound up living in Hawaii. I first came here in the Air Force, 1954. I was in the Air Force four years. And I came here not knowing anything, but in the military you go where you're sent.

I can remember during the early days of being here, this shows extreme ignorance on my part. We're driving around and I asked, "Hey man, where are the pineapple trees?" Oh, I don't know if I ever lived that one down. I never lived it down with me, that's for sure. I knew nothing about Hawaii because nobody ever taught me anything about Hawaii and I'd never studied it. But I fell in love with Hawaii.

Jeff: I hear you got into some trouble on the base.

Wally: One day I was going to work with two other friends, and we spotted this shapely blonde dressed in a white outfit. We were so pleased by what we were seeing, we acknowledged her with a couple of whistles. After we laughed at what we had done, I went for a test flight in a C-124. Upon my return, I was taken into custody by the Air Police. It seems the lady we had whistled at was the wife of an Air Policeman, who was also a native of Alabama, and he had not like the 'disrespect' shown his wife, for which I was singled out.

Therefore, I was harassed, threatened and told I had better watch my step on base. Also, I was told by the officer in charge of the Air Police I was not being singled out because of my color, only because of what I had done. I found that hard to believe since no one seemed to mind the two other airmen had also whistled.

With six months left, Wally believes to get even, they sent him to Guam to finish his service.

Wally: I transferred and I had not taken my GED test, so I didn't have a high school diploma yet. Before I got my discharge, I got my GED. And that officially made me a high school graduate, which opened doors that would've been closed otherwise. So, Hawaii was great.

The thing I've discovered with my life, and really with everybody's life, is that everything is connected. Just a giant puzzle. It's an amazing maze you grope your way through, doing your best to figure out where it's going and what's happening. And the thing I've come to understand, truly, it's going where it needs to go and it's going where it's best for me. And I need to accept that.

Be the best Wally I can and know that everything else will fall into place. I don't need to know what's going to happen next. Because my mantra is, "Let go and let God." And that's faith.

5

First Black Music Agent

Wally Amos has lived a life of "firsts". Rarely shying away from a new opportunity, he's been fortunate to blaze a trail built on taking chances.

Anyone who's ever done anything 'book-worthy' was confronted with an opportunity. Most likely, it was a situation they may not have been totally ready for. They may not have had the training...or contacts...or confidence. The most important trait they possessed, however, was courage to take a risk. They leaned-in to uncertainty and, many times, were handsomely rewarded. This theme dots the landscape of Wally's life.

When he was discharged from the Air Force, the opportunities weren't plentiful. He moved back to New York City and called a girl, Monya, he met while stationed in Hawaii. It's 1957. Wally's 21 and it was a call that would eventually change his life.

Wally: She was going to Collegiate Secretarial Institute, it was a business school. Took shorthand typing, that kinda of stuff, training to be a secretary. She recommended I go to school. Which is one of the best recommendations anyone ever made for me because I had no idea what I was going to do.

I was in electronics in the Air Force, repairing radios and radio sets on the airplanes, but I didn't want to do that. I didn't have a passion for it. So, Monya recommended Collegiate Secretarial Institute, and I did that.

I took Secretarial Courses: Math, Typing. Typing on manual typewriters. Computers, electronic stuff, had not been created then, you know. And the interesting thing, she got me a job at Saks Fifth Avenue. It was the first job I had out of the Air Force. It was just a menial job, unloading trucks and keeping the hallways clean at Saks Fifth Avenue.

The one thing I've always had, whatever assignment I was given, I always did the best I could. And that came directly from my mother, Ruby. Ruby was a taskmaster. If it wasn't your best, it was never acceptable to her. She was a high school dropout. She couldn't read, but she was a strong worker that would do anything and do it well.

And in those days, black people weren't trusted with anything. People wanted to watch my mom work and she stopped that immediately, because she was incredibly responsible and the best. That's why there was such a great demand for her work. She'd tell someone right up front, "Look if you're gonna be watching what I'm doing, then you got the wrong person. I'll go work for somebody else." They always yielded to her, because she was just that stature, man. There was just a sense about Ruby, "What a strong woman."

I was working at Saks Fifth Avenue, just unloading trucks and stuff. And what happened was, I got tired of doing that and I had been given the assignment to manage the Supply Department. Ernie Rikio, who was the manager, was moving to another department and I'd been one of the best workers in the department.

A guy named Vince Laberdi was in line for the managerial position. He knew he was gonna get it, because he was there when I got there. But Ernie Rikio gave it to me and I became the Manager. You know, 21 years old, whatever. And I took it very responsibly.

I did a really great job. I reorganized the whole department. I put everything in order. I mean, it's a huge place, but I had everything really tip-top shape. And so time went on and I was doing a good job managing the place.

I was friendly, knew everybody, everybody liked me. But I wasn't making any money then. My wife was pregnant, I had a child and I needed to make more money. So I asked Saks for a raise and they said they couldn't do it. I didn't know where I was gonna go, but I knew I was worth more than they were paying me.

The opportunity to work at the William Morris Agency showed up because the black organizations, NAACP and those groups, were applying pressure to the entertainment industry because a lot of the entertainers were black, especially in music and the Rock & Roll area. I quit Saks, and there was an opening at William Morris.

At the time, I was making I think, $75 a week at Saks. I'd asked for a raise up to $90 and they said, "No, man. We can't do that." I said, "Well, if you don't give me something, I'm gonna have to leave." They said, "No." So, I left.

I didn't have a job and ultimately I got a job at William Morris. I didn't know anything about show business. I mean, zilch. But I loved it. You start in the mail room. I went from $75 a week at Saks to $50 a week. But you know, I just thought, if it didn't feel right, I could never do it. And when Saks wouldn't give me a raise, I said, "That doesn't feel right."

They gave me the job at William Morris in the mailroom, making $50 a week. But you know, one thing that Ruby gave to me, "Be your best". If you're shining shoes, be the best shoe shiner. Whatever you're doing, just give everything you've got and be the very best you can be. And I took that to heart. And I still do. You know, 82 years old. If I'm going to be a shoe shine boy, I'll be the best.

I was told I would not receive special treatment because I was black and I would be judged solely on the quality of my work and attitude. I thought that was more than fair and was prepared to take them at their word.

I was in the mailroom, but some of the top agents in the company started in the mailroom. For instance, Irwin Winkler, who was in Television Packaging when I arrived and who later went on to produce such successful motion pictures as, "They Shoot Horses, Don't They?" And each of the Rocky films, starring Sylvester Stallone.

Also, a television agent named Bernie Brillstein who, when he left the WM Agency, became a personal manager and developed an important client list that included Jim Henson, Dan Aykroyd and more.

But, one of the biggest guys in the biz started in the mailroom. This guy would later become the head of a record label and movie studio. We got our start in the mailroom in the New York office of William Morris and have remained friends ever since. Today, he's worth at least a billion bucks. His name is David Geffen.

Jeff: At William Morris, how did you bring your A-game to the mail room?

Wally: The mailroom was the ultimate test and perfect training ground. We were the 'boys' of the organization. "Can I have a boy make a delivery to CBS?" "Can I have a boy to pick up some theater tickets at the Shubert Theater?" For me, it was a new experience being called 'boy' without the usual racial overtones accorded to black men.

In addition to our outside deliveries and pickups, our mailroom duties included picking up and delivering inter-office mail and sorting mail for delivery. Our duties also went as far as the lavatories, where we had to refill soap and hand towel dispensers and replace empty spools of toilet paper. And when lunch time arrived, we would relieve receptionists and secretaries.

As a matter of fact, it was while sitting-in for receptionists that I saw Abe Lastfogel, the legendary chairman of William Morris, who at that time was President, and who also started in the mailroom. In show business circles, Abe Lastfogel is a most respected name. In William Morris circles, it was a name you responded to immediately.

It was moments like that--seeing Abe Lastfogel and knowing from where he came--which also let me know show business was not all mail and toilet paper. It was, I quickly learned, a world where everybody wanted everything yesterday.

Working in the mailroom was a job that required you to listen, be observant, have initiative, plenty of patience, and do what you were told to do as quickly and efficiently as possible. It was also the perfect place to be to see how the agency functioned; you could literally see the business from the ground up. And seeing and meeting all the personnel of the company allowed me to draw my own conclusions and impressions of each one.

After several weeks, I started to feel comfortable enough to exert myself and show some initiative. During my first three weeks, I noticed the supplies and equipment, typewriters and adding machines, were desperately in need of some reorganization. Saks had provided me with expertise in this line of work, so I took it upon myself to clean and reorganize the entire area.

Lout Metz, the supervisor of the mailroom, was so impressed he turned the ordering and maintenance of the supplies over to me, which meant I would not have to make any outside deliveries or pickups.

In less than two months, my plan paid off. Between going to school at night and my typing practice during lunch, I acquired enough speed in typing and shorthand to be made a substitute secretary. It was a boost in ego and pay; another fifteen dollars a week.

My stay in the mailroom had been one of the shortest in the company's history.

Jeff: Where did you go from the mail room?

Wally: I got promoted to a William Morris trainee in the Rock & Roll division. You know, everything you do in your life, figures into your future. And you never know when you're going to use information you get. Because I had good typing skills, I had shorthand, I was perfect when they started the Rock & Roll division.

Ross was the head of it and she had her secretary she brought from the previous agency she'd been with. So, I became secretary to Ross's guy she brought over, called Jerry Brand, and I was his secretary.

You want to get better. You want to always improve whatever skills you have and you don't ever want to just lay lounging around, "That's good enough." It's never good enough, if you can do better and you want to always want to do better. I became an excellent secretary and eventually became the first African American agent at William Morris.

6

Wally's Famous Clients

When I met Wally Amos, I only knew about his famous cookie. Digging deeper into his life story, my jaw continued dropping. I had no idea he crossed paths with some of the biggest names in music. To me, his life before cookies was just as incredible. Check out the huge artists he discovered and/or managed...

Simon & Garfunkel

Wally: One of my earliest business relationships was with a tall, lanky, slow-talking black dude from Texas named Tom Wilson. We was a Harvard graduate, very bright and quite witty, and one of the two token black record producers at Columbia Records. Tom and I hit it off immediately, probably because we had a lot in common. We both had a sense of humor, were ambitious, liked music, and had a strong interest in the opposite sex.

It was meeting and getting to know Tom that first brought me into contact with two new singers named Paul Simon and Art Garfunkel.

Tom, who was producing Simon & Garfunkel, had been telling me all about them and how fantastic and different they were. One evening, I decided to stop by their recording session to check them out. The moment I saw them, I had to agree with Tom; they were unique in every way, most noticeably in their appearance.

Their first radio hit was 'The Sound of Silence' and Tom recorded that. He gave it little back beats, because that was his thing. He had just finished recording Bob Dylan and he added that kind of, little funky back beat stuff to 'The Sound of Silence', which is a very boring song. "Hello darkness, my old friend" (laughs). You know, Tom kind of jazzed it up and gave it a little more energy and a little more personality.

And as they say, the rest is history. It became a monumental hit record. And what happened along the way, the agents, my fellow agents, who --everybody had their own territory, and you book slots in your territory-- got so enamored with the name 'Simon & Garfunkel' and their appearance.

That song became a hit, and in the meantime, you have X number of days within your contract to get employment for whoever you represent. If you don't, they have the right to leave. William Morris had not done a good job. And I had done my best to get the other guys interested and to see the potential that was waiting there, but nobody would listen.

They decided not to sign with William Morris once they finally hit it big because the agency took too long to pull the trigger on them.

Jeff: I know you were a big believer in them and that must've have been a big loss for you and the agency. You even went so far to give Art Garfunkel some career-changing advice.

Wally: The two of them, Paul Simon and Artie Garfunkel. I've always believed in individuality. And we're all so unique, you know? Yet so many of us want to look like everybody else, but I never believed in that. I always believed in individuality. My God, Artie Garfunkel's hair was going every which way and Paul Simon looked like Napoleon. [Laughs]

There was a television guy who was a doctor and he looked like Artie Garfunkel, but his hair was one of his features. Art was thinking about cutting his hair and I told him, "Don't cut your hair. Why don't you let that be your signature?"

The thing that sustained them and made them a hit was their voices and Paul Simon's music. I mean it was phenomenal. That just lifted them up into super stardom because they were very consistent through the years. They just got bigger and bigger and bigger and then they didn't like each other and so they split up.

Jeff: Have you had any contact with them since those early days?

Wally: Very, very long time ago in the early days of Famous Amos, Paul Simon stopped by the cookie store one evening, just to say "Hello".

The Supremes

Wally: I was the first agent to book these ladies. Over 50 years ago, but actually, 1964, somewhere in there. I booked them on a Dick Clark tour. And Motown, Berry Gordy. Berry Gordy's sister, Esther Edwards. Esther ran the Management Division of Motown. And Esther had called us, and I was the liaison. We set up a meeting, she was coming to town and she wanted me to see. We weren't interested. We wanted to book Brenda Holloway.

Brenda Holloway had a record out called "Every Little Bit Hurts" and her record, honestly, she was smoking. We wanted Brenda Holloway and Esther Edwards was telling us about this new group they had coming out called The Supremes, and she played a record for us. This was their first record.

I booked The Supremes on their very first date, which was the Dick Clark Tour, filled with rock and roll acts. I went out on the tour with them. I've been on a lot of tours. But I remember when The Supremes played the Steel Pier in Atlantic City. All the rock acts played the Steel Pier, it was a legendary place.

We would play Tonk backstage with Diana Ross's mom. I can't remember her full name, but we called her Mrs. Ross. [chuckle] And we would play cards.

The Supremes, was one of the last records to have a hit record in Motown. And they were so pitiful, these little three raggedy girls, and they were backstage, man, and we'd play Tonk. [chuckles]

And they were, "Oh, we're never gonna have a hit record." And all of the older groups kind of adopted The Supremes. Nobody could touch the Supremes, because they really were their protector.

I remember when they came out on stage and Diana Ross, she was magic. And you knew eventually she had to split away from that group, because she was so clearly the focal point of the group. And eventually the group became Diana Ross and The Supremes. And then it became Diana Ross and she became a superstar.

Sam Cooke

Wally: I used to book the Apollo Theater and represented Sam Cooke, also traveled with him. A lot of the Rock & Roll acts during those years, they would be dancing all over the stage. Sam just had a magnetism. The ladies absolutely loved him and he would just stand there and slap his right leg. They would just fall out. He was a real super star. That voice was so special.

I used to travel on the road with him and he had a Cadillac. Always had a brand new Cadillac. I remember we were doing one night tours, one night stands and I drove the Cadillac. I think it was Raleigh, North Carolina to Atlanta, Georgia. Everybody else was tired after doing a gig. Wiped out you know, so I drove the car to Atlanta. I worked with a lot of Rock & Roll acts during those eras and it was fun.

Jeff: What happened to Sam Cooke?

Wally: A lady shot him. He was forcing himself on a female. He was a ladies man, you know, but he also didn't believe in "no". But no is no and he got shot.

Marvin Gaye

Wally: That's interesting because two acts that I worked with, Sam Cook and Marvin Gaye, got shot. I worked with Marvin early on and that worked out well for me in the early years because Marvin became one of the initial investors in Famous Amos Cookies. He's so gifted and so talented, but your ego gets you in trouble, man. He was arguing with his dad and his dad shot him. That's the epitome of stupidity, to argue with anybody.

But Marvin was an investor. I needed $25,000 and I think maybe Marvin put up $10k. He was one of the first investors in Famous Amos and I was in desperate shape when I was tracking him down and calling him to get some money.

I finally found him and we had a conversation. I'm ready to start selling cookies, and in a desperate situation and I'm almost begging and I'm frightened and I got this cookie company I've got to get going and Marvin said something that was very conformational after my cajoling and begging, he said, "Wally, if you're doing it, that's cool. I'll loan you the money." And he did.

It was a good lesson. If you've got character and accountability and people trust you, they'll help you if you're helping yourself. But, you're the most important person in your life. You and you alone have to really chart the course and you have to follow through.

Other acts Wally worked with: The Rolling Stones, Bobby Rydell, Bobby Vee, Gene Pitney, Brenda Holloway, Eric Burdon (The Animals) and Nancy Wilson (Heart).

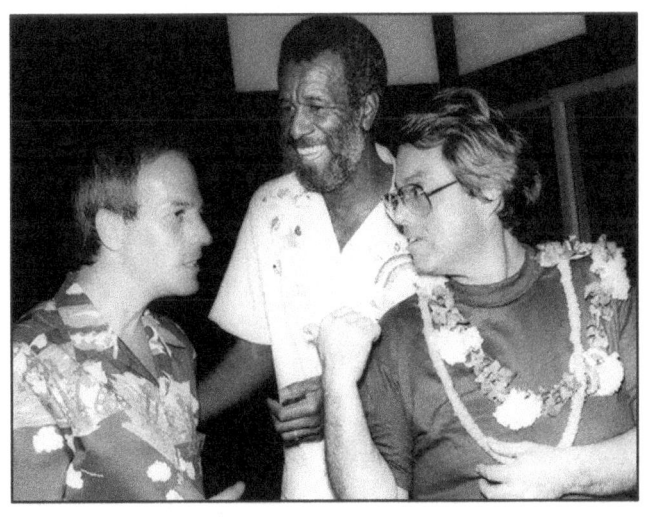

7

Hollywood Dreamin'

Wally: Around 1966, I began to get restless at William Morris. I had been booking Rock & Roll acts since 1962 and I was beginning to feel burned out. Also, the music was changing. We had entered the hard rock, or acid and psychedelic rock phase of music, and I was having difficulty relating to the loudness.

This was the era of Jefferson Airplane, The Grateful Dead, Canned Heat and the legendary Jimi Hendrix. A period that will probably be remembered as the most self-destructive in musical history, because performers were killing themselves through excessive use of drugs and alcohol.

At this point, Wally was second in charge in his division, behind Jerry Brandt. When Jerry left, he felt he should take his place as the Number One guy. William Morris didn't agree. They didn't give him the position, because, "it was felt the other agents wouldn't take direction from me because I was black." This was a paradox to Wally, "I was hired because I was black, and now I could not advance because I was black."

Wally leaves William Morris and heads West to start his own management company in Los Angeles, Wally Amos and Company. An industry executive bankrolled the venture to the tune of $110,000. Wally didn't waste anytime "investing" the money.

Wally: One of the first things I did was get an expensive wardrobe which cost me $2,500. I wanted to be the epitome of a person doing his 'show' thing. I didn't stop with the clothes, though. I also got an office in Beverly Hills; actually I got a larger office, since I was already sharing an office in Beverly Hills, and I rented some beautiful furniture.

In a way, all I was doing was being done without thinking clearly. Had I taken a moment to think about all these show things I was doing, I would have realized the only person who was going to benefit from all of this was me--my ego. The people I had to sell my clients to would not be coming to me, not yet anyway.

The next business within a business I formed was my own production recording company, called Lamplight Productions. This company I put in the hands of Mark Wildey, an Englishman I had met when I was at WM. Mark, at the time, was a road manager for the English Rock & Roll group, The Animals. I was getting ready to make a lot of money, although I was spending a lot of money, too.

In addition to the business life, I spent a lot of money to boost my personal life. We found this beautiful two story house in Hollywood. It was the nicest place I had ever lived up to the time. I really felt I had arrived.

About a year after launching the company, in 1969 it folded. Wally couldn't afford the Beverly Hills lifestyle any longer and had to move home and office into a one bedroom apartment in Hollywood.

Wally: Leaving my prestigious station in life in Beverly Hills, to go to my new and lower station, Hollywood, would have been more traumatic had I not remembered John Levy's parting and meaningful words when I left Venture Records, "Whatever you gotta do, you gotta do."

That was true this time as well, especially since I planned to continue being a personal manager. The facts were clear: I had to go where my money would take me.

Therefore, it would have to be the small apartment I found in Hollywood, on El Centro Avenue, which would also serve as my office. It was cheap, easy to manage, and quaint. I love the high ceilings of the huge living room and the single upstairs bedroom.

Once my friends saw my new apartment, they were quite envious, even though I didn't have any furniture. But that didn't bother me, just as this change was not the end of the world to me. I didn't sit around and feel sorry for myself, nor did I allow anyone else to. I had been here before--having nothing and trying to get something--and I had survived. Somehow I felt I would survive this time, too.

Getting settled at El Centro meant spending some money -- which I didn't really have -- toward home furnishings. I still needed carpet and music components, which were in my old Beverly Hills office. So, I decided I would go and get them, because, although I had broken my lease, I still had the keys. I went after my carpet and stereo equipment as soon as I could get a van and the person who installed the equipment went with me. It was done at night--with the van parked in the alley-- when no one else was around. I did it this way for the obvious reason, but I really didn't want anyone to see me make my final exit from a location and role I would play no more.

8

Captured by Cookies

Growing up, Wally's mother, Ruby, never made cookies. Her "desert platter" usually was adorned with pies and cakes. Before moving to New York to live with Aunt Della, his experience with the sweet treat was limited. Aunt Della is credited with planting the cookie seed. After leaving New York, chocolate chip cookies were mainly enjoyed as a memory.

In 1970, Wally represented Shari Summers, a young actress who played one of Harold's girlfriends in "Harold and Maude". She was also Mrs. Turner in "The Bad News Bears". If Aunt Della planted the cookie seed, Wally credits Shari Summers for watering it.

Wally: We finished our meeting and she busted out some chocolate chip cookies. I hadn't had any homemade cookies in a long time. My Aunt Della used to send them to me when I was in the Air Force. When I tasted them, memories just rushed to my head, and I said, "Shari, where'd you get these cookies from?" She said, "It's just the Nestle Toll House chocolate chip recipe."

I didn't believe her. But, what I really couldn't believe, was how long I deprived myself by not knowing about that recipe. I could bake. Had I known about the recipe, how complete my life would have been! I made up my mind, that evening I went to the market and picked up everything I needed, including Nestle's recipe and excitedly baked my first batch –ever- of chocolate chip cookies.

This radically rocked Wally's world. Now, cookies were a part of everything he did.

Wally: I'd go to meetings and would take cookies with me. I used cookies as my calling card, literally, and developed a nice reputation in Hollywood for making chocolate chip cookies that really tasted great!

I supplied Hollywood with cookies for a long time. One evening, I was having dinner with Quincy Jones' secretary, BJ Gilmore. She was really a neat lady; a lot of character and just a fine human being.

She said something no one had ever said before. She opened the door to where the prizes were hidden. BJ said, "You know, you and I should open a store selling chocolate chip cookies." I didn't even question it. It was one of those moments that, yes, it made so much sense.

Up until now, I just made them to share and developed a reputation for them. Every time people would see me, the first question would always be, "Hey man, where are my cookies?" Not, "Do you have any cookies today, Wally?" "Where are my cookies, man?" So this particular night, BJ says, "You ought to go in business selling cookies."

"That's a great idea, BJ, but I don't have the money." BJ thought she could get the money from a friend who was the owner of a well-known fast food franchise in Los Angeles called Tommy's Hamburgers. The idea of selling my cookies excited me.

Eventually, I said, "Okay." It was so natural. It seemed to be the thing to do. I woke up the next morning, and from then until now, that's all I thought about, was selling cookies. I'd never sold cookies. I made them for about five years, shared them with friends, but I never sold cookies. But I loved them.

From my days when Aunt Della made cookies for me, I absolutely loved chocolate chip cookies and still do. I love making them. There's just something magical about them. And I decided I would open a store selling chocolate chip cookies.

Since I had already told BJ to get busy locating her friend with the money, the next morning I was anxious to get started.

In less than five months, I'd gotten all the equipment, I got everything I needed. I know because I'd been making them for a while, so it was just common sense. I said, "I've been using a little of this, and then I'll just increase everything." And I put the whole thing together.

Clarence Tucker, a name that comes to mind, he worked for an equipment place. He was so helpful, such a fine human-being. He helped me find used equipment, and I had never ever done that before. But it was just common sense.

Hell, I'd made them at home for five years and I knew I needed an oven, I needed some bowls, I needed a mixer. I knew all the ingredients that I needed, so it was just basic stuff. And I was bitten by the bug, that's all I wanted to do after I made that decision to open a store, not a chain of stores. Not make a lot of money, but just open one store and sell chocolate chip cookies.

9

Wally's Famous Friends
Save His Cookie

K nee deep in pulling together pieces for the store, BJ
Gilmore grinds the brakes on Wally's momentum
when she reveals her friend can't invest in the business.
Sure, it stung, but in true Wally-fashion, he shook it off
and started knocking on famous friends' doors for
money.

Wally: I didn't intend to quit now. I loved the idea too
much, including the possibility of eating chocolate chip
cookies whenever I pleased, while making a living at the
same time.

Wally bakes up a crazy business plan to present to possible investors.

Wally: It was December, 1974 and all my notes for the
proposal were ready. The fourteen pages of creative writing flowed easily and I was entertained while typing it. I

hoped whoever read it would also be just as entertained and tempted enough to take a bite. Actually, that was a literal possibility, because at the opening of the proposal was a package of various cookies--chocolate chip with pecans, chocolate chip with peanut butter and butterscotch chip with pecans--which I planned to sell.

In addition to giving the potential investor an opportunity to get a taste of what they'd be putting their money into, I felt they should understand my sense of humor and maybe get a good laugh as well. After all, how many serious proposals are also capable of making the investor laugh? I also placed cookies at the end of the proposal so readers finished up laughing and wanting more of my chocolate chip cookies.

Investors of the original Famous Amos Cookie store included:

-Helen Reddy, Singer & Jeff Wald, Manager |
Invested $10,000

Wally: When I met with Jeff at his home, I started to give him a full sales pitch--something I had been preparing myself to do for the last three months--but he cut me off, telling me I didn't need to sell him or Helen. They knew me, and that was enough. With that attitude, I decided to ask him for the entire budget of $25k.

Jeff said all he could go for was $10k, because his business manager, whom he listened to, was not positive about his investing in chocolate chip cookies as he was. The truth was, Jeff and Helen were investing in me because I was their friend. Their desire to see me succeed was the reason for investing.

-Artie Mogull, President, United Artists Records
Discovered Bob Dylan, Olivia Newton John and Hootie and the Blowfish | Invested $5000

Wally: Artie Mogull put up $5,000 and his check bounced, but he ultimately came through and I got the money.

-Marvin Gaye, Singer | Invested $10,000

Wally: I called Marvin to give him a sales pitch and he cut me off, "That's cool, you don't have to do that. I know you, Wally, and it's okay. I'm in for $5k."

As the launch date quickly approaches, Wally's still short on cash. He makes another call to Marvin to ask for an additional $5000.

Wally: However, Marvin had a different hat on this time. He was now the businessman. He wanted to know if he was going to get a larger percentage for his $10k.

Marvin also knew time was running out for me and he was in a good position to negotiate. I can't blame him-- friendship aside, this was business. So I gave him the extra points because I needed his money. I figured a smaller percentage of something was better than a larger percentage of nothing.

-Oscar Brown, Jr. Jazz Singer | Contributed the name.

Wally: I was managing Oscar Brown, Jr. He was an exceptionally talented...a legendary jazz singer. Very bright guy, wonderful entertainer. The birthplace of that name was in Washington DC, during one of Oscar's performances. After Oscar's performance many fans showed up backstage to wish him well, many knew and spoke to me. After a while my popularity was noticed by Oscar, who responded, "Damn, Famous Amos!"

Just throwing it away like that. But, at that time, we were looking for a name. Famous Amos was a natural. There it was. What else were you going to do with it? There are so many moments in life like that, where it doesn't require a second thought, because the first one is so prominent and powerful.

10

Unveiling the Famous Cookie

Wally: When I decided to do this, I started looking for a location. And this building that had been a pie joint on Sunset and Formosa, I'd walk by that building every day, and I mean it was so perfect.

I called Ellen Collum, a lady who was helping me with secretarial stuff, and said, "Ellen, go by that store on Sunset and Formosa, it's a pinball operation. Go by there and check it out." The day she went by, those guys were jumping out of their lease.

I said, "It's an incredible location. Great billboard up there, right on Sunset Boulevard, thousands of cars go by every single day." I talked Bud Barish, owner of Barish Chrysler who owned the building, into letting me rent the space. There was a guy named Chuck Cassell. Chuck Cassell worked with me at A & M Records and was a close friend. He was a talented writer.

Chuck didn't think it was a good location. He thought it was bad luck due to the failure of so many other businesses. "Now tell me Chuck, how can a corner, this corner, be bad luck? The corner didn't do anything to anyone. This corner was meant to house a cookie cottage. I can just see it." Thousands of cars pass that location every single day! I thought it was a great... And it was.

I decided to use that location on Sunset Boulevard and put a sign in the window: The cookies are coming! The cookies are coming! March 9th.

I knew all the stuff, I knew all the equipment, I just needed bigger equipment. So, I found everything I needed and opened the first chocolate chip cookie store in the world. I opened that March 9th, 1975, on the corner of Sunset and Formosa.

Jeff: Here you are, a black man starting a business in American in 1975. How rare was it to achieve such success at that time in our history?

Wally: In the '70s, there were a lot of black men in business. There weren't a lot of them selling cookies though, white ones either. There were bakeries, but there weren't any stores selling just chocolate chip cookies. I was the first one to do that. And I never thought about the color of my skin.

I never thought about NOT being able to do it. I was focused on opening a store and selling cookies. Yeah. I mean, laser-beam focus. And everything I did, I did to help achieve my goal of opening a cookie store. And, I mean, the first one to sell just chocolate chip cookies. So, I just needed to open that store.

Jeff: It's March 8th, 1975...the night before opening day. What was happening?

Wally: I still had to mix the cookie dough and it was like 7:00, 8:00 at night by then. I'm opening the next day, and I'm the only one that knows how to mix the cookie dough. And I just started. I had never made cookie dough in the bakery. I think it was about 1,400 square feet of space. But you know, most things you do in life, you do for the first time. If life is anything, it is trial and error.

The opening of my first case of pecans was a very special moment. When I bought pecans in the supermarket they were in small 2 ¾ ounce packs Now I had a 30-pound case, and when I opened it, I put my hands down into the pecans and let them trickle through my fingers like gold nuggets. What a great moment this was, having all of these pecans at my disposal.

After measuring everything out--with me happy as a lark, singing, having a good time, and totally in my glory-

-I mixed my batter in this 60-quart mixer bowl. After that, I had to get the dough on the baker's tray. At home, I did it with a teaspoon, which I had to do on this occasion as well. So there I was, measuring out dough with a teaspoon, one cookie at a time and placing them on this 18 x 27-inch baker's tray, which held 120 cookies. Then it was placed on a rack until enough trays were accumulated to go into the oven.

The slow process went on all night. Friends would stop by to give me words of encouragement. Then, about 5 am, I stopped baking the butterscotch chip cookies with pecans, which I had started first, because the chocolate chip cookies with pecans were the product--the premium cookies--which everyone would be looking for.

About 8 or 9 am, my people arrived at the shop, and after I instructed them in the baking of the cookies, I took my weary body--I had been going so long, I didn't know how tired my body was--to the nearest Jacuzzi and steam room at The Beverly Hills Health Club to energize it.

After the health club, I returned to the store and this little kid who was the son of a really famous writer from the LA Times asked for my autograph. I just laughed. I couldn't stop laughing. "What do you want my autograph for?" I booked a lot of entertainers, but I'm not one of them. Now with the opening of the store, I had elevated to a different class. And it was a realization things were going to change a little bit, and they did, they changed a hell-of-a lot. That was a funny moment. I've been working so hard to get this stuff together, and this young man asked for my autograph. I just started laughing.

Jeff: Since you didn't have much money, how did you promote the grand opening?

Wally: I didn't have any money for advertising, but I knew everyone at studios, the record companies, so I got envelopes and with the generous help from my talented friends in the Graphics Department at A&M Records, made an invitation for the grand opening. I would hand-deliver them, because I didn't have money for postage. So, I delivered them to television studios, record companies and just created tremendous word-of-mouth.

Wally blanketed Hollywood with 2500 invitations and even created a slick headshot for his newest client, The Cookie.

Wally: Something I realized right away, I wasn't really leaving show business, nor would I be giving up all my personal management clients. Not with The Cookie, which I had already called, to tease the public, "The Superstar of Cookies". To establish the fact it had to be promoted very well, I realized I would have to manage The Cookie just as I would any other client. Why not?

After almost fourteen years as an agent and personal manager, if I couldn't do what was necessary to make my cookies the superstars I knew they were, then no one could.

Jeff: Tell me about the big day...the grand opening of the world's first chocolate chip cookie store, Famous Amos Cookies.

Wally: We stopped traffic on Sunset Boulevard. It was a monumental opening. People started coming from everywhere. They were calling from the airport to see how they could pick some up. I mean those cookies became the rage. They were just everywhere. People loved them, and they still do. They still do.

It was the Must Attend party of 1975. Over 1500 turned out to taste Hollywood's newest star. The party was complete with free champagne, valet parking and a band. As the news cameras were rolling, Wally grabbed the mic...

"It is un-American, not to like chocolate chip cookies! We need to them to sustain ourselves, you know? Right! To get from one day to the next, in this world of frustrations and wars and fights, we need chocolate chip cookies, so we can all come together, and have a good time, right?"

Jeff: How surprised were you by the turnout?

Wally: Oh, I was surprised, but I wasn't really surprised. The cookies tasted good and I'd been giving them away for five years. I knew there was a formula there. And I knew the product was superior to any chocolate chip cookie. And no one was selling just chocolate chip cookies. I was the first person to ever do that.

11

The Cookie Business

J eff: At the time, what were your competitors selling?

Wally: I had no competitors. There were people selling chocolate chip cookies in bakeries and stuff, but there was no one that sold just chocolate chip cookies. And I had a butterscotch, I had oatmeal, but there was no one who that did that. I was the first person who did that.

Jeff: That was risky not to have a cookie business model in place where you had examples of others...

Wally: But I didn't know about a business model, and that's stuff people make up. I had five years of testing. I'd been giving cookies away for five years and built a reputation within the Entertainment Industry for making the best tasting chocolate chips ever. And I decided to sell them. It wasn't a giant step. It was just common sense.

That was the next thing to do. And people came from everywhere to try them. I mean, it was magical. It was great.

Jeff: Talk to me about the first year of business.

Wally: It was a heavy time. I was everywhere. I was thinking of ways to sell, create exposure, I was just doing everything I could to get attention and to let people taste them, because it's always been about taste. It still is. You got to taste them before you know whether you like them or not, and you can't fool your mouth.

That's an early quote I created, because you can't trick your mouth. If something tastes good, your mouth's going to want more and more and more of it. And that's all I did, was just give samples out. I had a yellow Volkswagen Bug with graphics all over it.

But I'm a promoter, that's all I am, really. If you don't promote what you got, then how are people going to know what it is? And you got to give samples away if it's food so they can taste it. That was just basic stuff, man. That's not brain science. I'd walk up to anybody, "Here, have a cookie." Word-of-mouth is still the best way to sell a product, especially food. Let people taste it.

In Hollywood, I was hiring unemployed actresses to go to stores and give cookies away on Sunset Boulevard, throughout Beverly Hills. And then I would deliver them in my yellow Volkswagen Bug. I'd have my kazoo going, "Cookies here. Cookies here!" But show business was who I was. The one thing I knew how to do was promote. And I promoted the way Wally promoted, not the way somebody else promoted.

I've always done what I do, and it caught on. But word-of-mouth, word-of-mouth is the absolute most powerful form of advertising, whatever you're selling, 'cause if people catch on to it, they'll tell everybody, and that's what happened. And I started doing media stuff, television, radio stuff, I was the talk of the land.

Jeff: What was it like to go from being a promoter to being the promoted?

Wally: I soon found I would have to get physically involved with the fun I was creating on behalf of Famous Amos. Initially, there were magazine articles and television interviews after the Hollywood store opened. It finally got to the point when I wasn't only the promoter. I was the promoted. Therefore, I had to resolve, "I am Famous Amos! If I don't promote The Cookie, who will?"

However, that grand decision was not without anxieties. First, I had never been in the spotlight. I was always in the background when handling my clients, but my new client was different: It was necessary for me to be out front and I had no choice.

Then, I discovered I was entertaining. So I started projecting more of myself. I performed like I was onstage; you know, the delivery, the ideas. I was suddenly a total creative being. Why not? All the funny put-ons were from me and were my own concepts and creations. Also, if I didn't do it, it would never happen.

1975 was a good year to open the world's first cookie store. Wally moved $300,000 in cookies, but he didn't realize much profit.

Wally: By August 1975, my income at the store still hadn't picked up, but my publicity had.

But, he was spending a lot. On August 17, 1975, he opened a second store in Tarzana, CA and a third in Tucson, AZ on May 9, 1976.

In 1976, a friend took some cookies to the execs at Bloomingdale's in New York. They loved them and wanted to meet the man behind the cookie.

Wally: The meeting was between two haughty people. Me, because I had all of this publicity and felt I was very important, and Gumport, because he had been the connoisseur of gourmet foods at Bloomingdale's for over 30 years. When I arrived his attitude was, "Just who does this guy think he is?"

The first thing out of his mouth was, "I've tasted the cookies and I think they're too dry. I don't think they're so hot." My response was immediate and final, "Then you don't have to buy them," and I got up to leave. But Gumport stopped me and decided we should talk.

And I later learned, Gumport was only the first line of fire. He screened me first, then James Schoff, Jr., Executive VP was called in. We went over the same things I had said to Gumport, who interjected several negative remarks from time to time.

Finally, I got tired of it and said, "Look, if you guys don't want the cookies, that's okay. You don't have to buy them. I'll just leave." Schoff stopped me, and we talked longer; enough so when I left Bloomingdale's I had a deal to sell Famous Amos cookies there. Now my problems really began.

In order for Wally to sell cookies at department stores throughout the country, he had to ramp up production. He opened a factory in Nutley, NJ to satisfy demand. A serious Famous Amos craze was sweeping the nation. The cookies were regarded as The Cookie of The Jet Set and the first Celebrity Cookie.

In 1977, Wally drops Bloomingdale's for Macy's, a brilliant marketing move! His cookies would now be on parade, for 20 million television viewers.

Wally: I did the Macy's Thanksgiving Day Parade for seven years in a row, I think. I'd been raised in New York, and went to the parade as a kid, and my children, I took to the parade, and now here I am, in the parade, man! It was so cool!

Eventually, Wally expands distribution to Nieman Marcus department stores and a promotional event at their Dallas store was unforgettable.

Wally: The Cookie and I were arriving on a Brink's armored truck. I rode on the running board of the truck. At the entrance to Neiman Marcus, the guard, which had his hand firmly on his gun, removed the cookies, which were in silver bags, and carried them into the store--still with his hand on his weapon--and placed these precious morsels in a roped-off window area where the Famous

Amos Boutique had been set up; the highlight of which was our logo in neon.

By 1979, Wally was in command of a massive operation. The factories were churning out 7,000 pounds, of cookies every day. By 1982, revenues hit 12 million. He was a household name, he had his own TV show, and was on a lot of others.

In 1981, Wally was a guest on Taxi, when Latka inherits his grandmother's cookie recipe and wants to make his as good as Famous Amos. The big problem? Latka's cookies contain an addictive drug.

In 2012, he appeared an episode of The Office, entitled "Tallahassee", as himself. He also was on The Jeffersons, Oprah and more!

From a Famous Amos Commercial:

"I'm on your refrigerator, I'm in your pantry, I'm in your desk drawer, I'm in a supermarket, I'm in convenience stores, I'm in department stores, I'm in service stations, I'm in airports, I'm on television! That's what makes Amos Famous."

In 1980, Wally's trademark hat and shirt were inducted into the Smithsonian's Business Americana Collection. Turns out, Wally was the first African-American businessman, to be represented in the collection. Minor detail, it was Wally who sold the idea to the Smithsonian. What Wally lacked in business experience, he made up for in promotional exuberance. He was a marketing maniac.

Wally: I can promote anything if I have a connection to it. If I can feel it inside of me, then I can bring it to life, and I can explain it to someone else. I can help someone else see it and like it. I never wanted to need anybody, and I never do. It's kind of to throw you off balance, but in a fun way.

Effort is highly underrated. Effort is what gets you over the top, man. Effort is where that little extra ounce of energy you need to pop the creativity in your head, to give you the answer when you're just searching because things are happening so fast, and you're just moving to get cookies moving or whatever your business is.

People Magazine proclaims Famous Amos, "The Best Chocolate Chip Cookie in America" in 1983. Wally tells People, "I don't think I could do it just for the money...I always said one day I'd have a big star, and this is it.

It loves me, takes care of me. It's the all-time great per-
former."

12

Wally's Cookie Crumbles
(Sorry, had to be done)

I n 1986, President Reagan honored Wally with one of the first Entrepreneurial Excellence Awards. I don't think anyone told Ronnie, but a year before, in 1985, Wally's company had lost $300,000. Revenues were slipping and Wally's empire crumbling. Every time investors would step in to supposedly help, Wally lost more equity and control of it.

Wally: There is tremendous satisfaction in doing something people really enjoy, that I enjoy, that I have great pride in doing. A job well done! I did a good job developing it and did a piss-poor job losing it. I wasn't always responsible. I was never a business guy, though. I never knew the dynamics of business. I never took the time to learn. And by the time I figured it out, I'd lost the company.

Jeff: What's an example of behavior you exhibited during Famous Amos that wasn't best for the company?

Wally: I just thought I was in charge. I thought I knew everything. I thought I was hot shit. And with that attitude, you discover you're not. Clearly, because you have so much success and people singing your praises and telling you this and that, it's not true; but you didn't have the insight or the depth to realize it. So you do a lot of stupid things that massages your ego and you're not your ego, you got to go deeper.

Every part of it is critical to your growth and I quit using phrases like, "I wish I had done this", or "I should have done that." Because you learn from what you learn and then you just make those internal changes that are necessary and start living at a higher level, instead of doing the same things.

Jeff: You admitted you were more into the show than into the business.

Wally: Yes. I wasn't capable. I've never been a numbers guy. I've never been the business guy to calculate the cost. I can't do that. I've never wanted to do that. I'm the guy that can promote it though.

I needed people that knew the business and understood the business and could operate within the business. I never could and I pretended I could because I had the final say. I made some really horrible decisions. They didn't help me, but in one way or another, caused me to lose the company because I thought I knew everything.

Life is a learning experience and we all die. Everything's a learning experience if that's what you make it. But I'd just come to the conclusion that whatever happens is absolutely supposed to happen, because if it weren't, something else would have happened.

Between 1985 and 1988, Famous Amos went through four different owners. Each had their own strategy to save the company. From licensing the Famous Amos brand to candy, hot chocolate, ice cream and soda...all failed.

A decade after launching the world's first cookie store, being dubbed the Father of the Gourmet Cookie, Wally was merely a contract employee, pitching the very cookie, that launched a revolution. By 1988, Famous Amos had lost 2.5 million dollars, and The Shansby Investment Group, picked it up for three million. Incredibly frustrated, Wally walks away a year later.

Jeff: How do you think things may have been different if you were more of a numbers guy, more focused on the bottom line?

Wally: But I'm the one who started the company. I don't play those tricks. If I had been, you'd never know. There are no answers to any of those questions. If I was a different person, how would it have played out if I was Chinese instead of African American?

Jeff: But, numbers are business.

Wally: But I've never been good with numbers, so I've never ... That's not been my forte. I've always made sure that, whenever I could, I had somebody that understood the numbers. I could make you laugh. I could give you great service, but I can't dissect numbers for you. I can't make this number or this cookie be more or be profitable or ... Maybe I could make it be profitable, just to make sure it tastes good all the time because the only requirement a cookie has is to taste good. When a customer bites down in a cookie, the only thing that matters is that that cookie tastes good.

Jeff: If you're giving them away for free, yes.

Wally: No, even if you're selling them.

Jeff: Numbers matter, though.

Wally: Yeah, numbers matter, but if you're selling them and they don't taste right and they're not right, then you're going to get bad numbers. That's common sense.

Jeff: Look at the flip side. Famous Amos today, and a lot of people say this, and I know you agree ... they don't taste like they used to.

Wally: No, its just empty flour and sugar and blah. There's no heart, you taste the machine, you taste the robot ... robot cookies!

Jeff: But they're still making a lot of money.

Wally: Because they don't taste like the original doesn't prove you can't sell them for cash. Big deal. I don't want to sell a product that doesn't taste good, especially if it's supposed to taste good, and food is supposed to taste good. Now, I can sell a horrible cookie to somebody five, six, seven, eight, nine, maybe ten times, but it's going to fade off after a while because you can't fool your mouth. So, quality matters.

Jeff: Definitely. How does that sit with you today that your name is on a package with cookies that don't taste like your original recipe?

Wally: If people like it, they like it. I have no control over that cookie at all and have not for a long, long time, and I don't give a damn what it tastes like. Not my business. My business, let's see if I can come back one more time with a cookie that tastes the way I want it to taste, and then that one won't even exist, because, in food, taste is king.

If mine tastes good, you're not goanna want that one just because it's a name. You can't eat the name. You can only eat the product. If you like the way the taste product, nothing else matters. Give me some taste. Yeah, give me some taste.

The Shansby Group turned the business around by slashing manufacturing costs and ending licensing deals. They lowered the price in order to compete with cookies like Nabisco's Chips Ahoy and Keebler's Chips Deluxe. BUT their big play was to do something Wally didn't.

Until now, Famous Amos wasn't widely available in supermarkets. Shansby needed widespread distribution to save the iconic cookie. Keep in mind, it's the late 80s. Membership stores were thriving. They saved a ton of money on advertising and distribution by getting Famous Amos into –these- club stores. And their final play...YOU probably have experienced...they started selling the cookie in vending machines.

Less than a year after launching the new strategy, in 1991, sales were up to 42 million and operating income hit 4.5 million.

Holding the company long term was never Shanby's goal. They wanted to quickly breath dollars back into the battered brand and flip it.

Flush with chips, in 1992, they sell to President Baking for $61 million. 9 years later, Kellogg's picks it up and in 2019 sells the company Wally started in 1975 with $25k in loans from Marvin Gaye and other famous friends-...they sell Famous Amos and the Keebler brand for $1.3 billion.

Today, the cookie biz has never been sweeter. Yearly, the US consumes $6.1 BILLION of the tasty treats.

13

Cookie Wars:
Lawsuits and Limitations

P robably the most damning part of losing Famous Amos, was Wally losing the right to use his name or image to promote any future baked good company. When Wally left in 1989, he signed an agreement which stated he no longer owned his God-given name and image in regards to the cookie business. I believe this has been one of the biggest road blocks to Wally ever achieving another big hit.

The cookie space is insanely crowded. Standing out is difficult. Imagine how much easier it would be if Wally were able to say, "Hey, it's me Wally Amos. I'm the guy who created the cookie you used to love, Famous Amos. Well, I'd like for you to try my new cookie." Under the terms of the agreement, it's impossible to tell that story. Despite the agreement, in 1992, Wally launches a new cookie business called "Wally Amos Presents: Chip &

Cookie". His wife, at the time, designed two dolls named: Chip & Cookie. The idea was to re-enter the market place with a total package: cookies, dolls, t-shirts, books and other merchandising material.

Before Wally can sell his first batch, The Shansby Group sues and charges Amos with unfair competition and trademark infringement. They said Wally signed agreements in 1985 & 1986 giving the company the rights to his name. A federal judge in 1992 bared Amos from using his name, likeness, voice or signature to sell the new cookies. Amos countersued, claiming breach of contract.

Most people assume they have a right to their own legal name, but not in business.

Colonel Harland Sanders, the white-suited pitchman of Kentucky Fried Chicken tried to open another restaurant, The Colonel's Lady Dinner House, after selling his chicken chain in 1964. The new owners filed a lawsuit claiming an infringement on its trademark rights. The Colonel countersued for $122 million for allegedly interfering with his attempts to franchise restaurants. Both parties ended up dropping their cases. Wally wasn't so lucky.

The judge issued orders barring him from using the four names in any future baking business: Wally Amos, Famous Amos, Famous and Amos!

Keith Lively, president of Famous Amos at the time, said his company had the sole right to the commercial use of all those names. More than just the names, they also owned the right to his voice and image. "He (Amos) has to get involved in an industry where he can't create confusion in the mind of the public," Lively said. "He can sell satellite dishes. He can sell microchips. He just can't sell cookies, or (if he does) not promote them himself."[1]

One of Wally's demands in the legal settlement was for "the company" to remove the claim from its cookie bags that it still uses Famous Amos' original recipe. They agreed.

That's been a massive hurdle and is probably one reason Wally's struggled ever since. BUT, to be fair, he signed the agreement.

Jeff: At the time you were signing that and you saw that clause, what'd you think?

Wally: I didn't think anything. I didn't give it any credence, really. I was not a good steward. I wasn't in control, other people were making decisions. I made wrong decisions.

Jeff: Have you ever explored the opportunity to reverse that, to regain control of your name?

Wally: I never had the money to hire an attorney to really look at it, because I think the life of that first agreement only had 10 years to go because that's the limit in California. And I've never been able to get the money to really hire someone to dig up that old agreement and look at it and see what it was. So, it's conceivable that agreement is not even effective anymore. But there are a lot of other names you could use and we'll just do that.

Who I am is so much greater than the name "Wally Amos". I'm not attached to it. I can use my personality to create more things and make more money.

Google "Unflappable Persistence" and if a picture of Wally Amos DOESN'T come up, call Al Gore (inventor of the internet) and demand change. Despite the road-blocks, Wally's hunger for cookies and entrepreneurship hasn't wavered. Can't use his name? So what? Try another one. Oh, he tried over ten different names throughout the decades.

A partial list of cookie companies since the fall of Famous Amos:

- Chip & Cookie
- SOMA
- Uncle Noname
- Wamos
- The Cookie Guy
- The Cookie Man
- Cookie Kahuna
- Uncle Wally's
- Cookie Kahuna

After the lawsuit, Wally launched "Uncle Noname" (pronounced "no-NAH-may") as a tongue-in-cheek response to his loss.

Wally: Uncle Noname, was "no name", sounded like Japanese, but it just said no name. Because there's always a way you do it, you know, and sometimes it's painful, but I made it fun. You can't cry over spilled milk. You can't cry, or regret what you don't have, you got to do something different.

Jeff: 40 years ago, did you think at 80, you'd still have to be moving this much...working this hard?

Wally: I've been moving for a long time. I'm actually tired of moving. You know, it's just, -phew-, a lot of stuff. But there's something inside of me, I mean, what'll I do if I quit? You know, stay in this room? I mean, that's not an option, man, no. Not an option at all. So you got to keep going.

I've never thought about what I would be doing in the future, because I've been so busy doing what I'm doing now. There is no future. The only time is now. And all I do is take care of now. More now than I did before, because I didn't understand that concept before. But now I know truly how important now is.

And it's always now. You can't get out of now. I don't care how much it hurts, how much pain ... it doesn't matter. You can't leave now. "When I get" ... When, when, when, when. No. No. There is no "when". There's now. And if you're not taking care of now, to some degree of responsibility, then you're dead.

In a 1994 interview, when asked about the future of Uncle Noname Cookies, Wally said, "We projected that by 1996, we'll be grossing $27 million."[2] Unfortunately, competition in the cookie space was fierce and Uncle Noname couldn't keep up.

Wally: "It was just an uphill battle, looking to establish a new cookie company without having the resources and still in the minds of everybody being Famous Amos."[3]

When debt surged to $1.3 million, Wally filed for Chapter 11 bankruptcy protection in 1997. Two years later, he emerges with a fresh spirit and idea: low-fat and fat-free muffins. Under the terms of a new deal with Keebler, the owner of Famous Amos at the time, he wrestled back the rights to use his name to sell muffins and Uncle Wally's was born.

Additionally, the Keebler Company offered Wally a two-year contract to do what he does best, promote the brand he built. In 1999, he started a promotional tour to celebrate the 25th anniversary of Famous Amos Cookies. Wally was back in front of TV cameras doing what was baked into his DNA.

While Uncle Wally's muffin company, or any other venture, didn't last long, it wasn't for the lack of passion. No one is more passionate about providing tasty treats to the public. Spreadsheets and business plans be damned, Wally's always prioritized the human connection his wares create. If one of his signature cookies can produce a smile from a customer, that's a boost to his spiritual bottom-line.

14

The Great Cookie Comeback

What a wild ride! The life of Wally Amos is a dizzying display of twists and turns.

Today, at 85, Wally still hustles to regain the throne to the cookie kingdom. When we first met in 2015, he was about a year away from being homeless. Of course, he/we didn't know it at the time. How could we have? He was busy promoting his latest cookie company, Cookie Kahuna, on Shark Tank. All signs pointed to success.

The new company fueled our desire to document the experience. How many former business icons try their hand at writing a fresh chapter at age 80? The story was engaging. Who doesn't want to root for Wally? His optimism and positive spirit are infectious and uplifting.

Despite valleys outnumbering the peaks in his life, Wally's been able to maintain his 1000-watt smile…at least outwardly. And when he flashes that smile, it's hard not to crack one of your own.

So, we grabbed some cameras and started rolling on the life of the charismatic cookie entrepreneur. The result is the documentary, "**The Great Cookie Comeback: reBaking Wally Amos**".

If you're interested in finding out what happens with Cookie Kahuna, Shark Tank, a fifth marriage, homelessness, health scares and, of course, a rich history of cookies and trail blazing, we'd love for you to pick up the story in the doc.

Since you invested time in page-flipping through Wally's story, we'd love to offer a special discount to see the film. Please check out the Free Offer after this chapter for some sweet freebies!

Jeff: How important is legacy?

Wally: Legacy to me is not important. It's what you do now. It's not what you leave, it's how you treat people. It's the giving that you have shared with others. It's the concern that you have for other people. Don't remember me, it doesn't matter. I don't do anything to be remembered by.

No, I do things to help people. To make the world a better place for somebody, and for me. And so, I've never been concerned about legacy. No, man, I'll be gone, so it won't mean anything for me. If somebody can remember me in a favorable way, that's cool. Yeah, that would be nice.

Jeff: How about the legacy of your superstar cookies?

Wally: I think there's a piece of me in every cookie anybody's ever bit down on, because I AM these cookies. They are a part of me. I am a part of them. That's the bottom line.

I've never felt as lost in as just falling into a situation as I often have with just coming in touch with my cookies. And meeting someone who has such positive comments and such an incredible look on their face because of my cookies, which are MY cookies.

All things belong to God. I'm so blessed that God saw fit to bring these cookies into existence through me, through my head, through my ideas, through my Aunt Della. This person made chocolate chip cookies for me when I was 12 years old. I'm 85 years old now. Wow. It's a lot of cookies. A lot of cookies.

Jeff: What do you want the name 'Wally Amos' to mean?

Wally: He was a nice person. Wally Amos was a caring human being. He cared about other people. He cared a lot. He was here to serve others and he made a really great cookie.

[Wally looks off camera for a couple seconds, silently reviewing his life, and then turns back.]

No question about it.

References

[1] Forbes, 12/20/93 "Famous, Shmaymous" William Heuslein p. 146

[2] Business in Broward, 4/94 "His Cookie Crumbled, So Amos Made a Better Cookie" Sherry Friedlander p. 7

[3] The New York Times, 7/3/99 "A Famous Cookie And a Face to Match; How Wally Amos Got His Hand And His Name Back in the Game" Dana Canedy

Free Offer

To show our thanks for spending time getting to know Wally, we'd love to share some free stuff!

-Wally's Famous Cookie Recipe

-Fun Wally Amos Meme

-Book of Wally's Positivity Quotes

-20% Coupon Code for Cookie Lovers Film Package

Grab 'em while they're hot!

www.GreatCookieComeback.com/BookFreebies

About the Author

Jeff MacIntyre is passionate about finding and telling stories that matter. His Los Angeles-based production company, Content Media Group, has been producing broadcast and documentary content for over two decades.

50 countries and 18 Emmy Awards later, Jeff believes everyone has a rich story and loves traveling the world to tell them.

Get in touch! jeffmac@ContentMediaGroup.com

Thank You!

Thanks again for checking out **Cookie King, Wally 'Famous' Amos**. I hope you enjoyed learning about Wally's incredible life story. As you know, reviews are super important for small time publishers, like us. Your positive review could help others discover this book.

To leave a review, simply log-in to your Amazon account and locate this book in your orders. Go to the book's page and scroll down to write a customer review.

Thanks SO much! Wally and I greatly appreciate it!